Hurry Up, America, & Spit

OTHER BOOKS BY PEARL BAILEY

The Raw Pearl
Talking to Myself
Pearl's Kitchen
Duey's Tale

Hurry Up, America, & Spit

Pearl Bailey

HARCOURT BRACE JOVANOVICH
NEW YORK AND LONDON

Printed in the United States of America

First edition

Library of Congress Cataloging in Publication Data

Bailey, Pearl.
    Hurry up, America, & spit.

    1. Bailey, Pearl.   I. Title.
ML420.B123A28   081   76–12481
ISBN 0-15-143000-4

B C D E

Hurry Up, America, & Spit

THE OCEAN IS LOVE

The ocean is love.
It gently gathers itself and heads for the shore.
Somewhere along the way a wave decides to
    separate and go alone
To crash the shore.

The sands mingle as people,
Sorting each other out like people.
This one subsides. This stands out.

Waves saying hello and goodbye.
Do they head back out?
Rejoin the vastness of the deep?

In, out. Out, in.
The waves come in short, angrily,
And whisper.

SOMEHOW, GOING BACK

Somehow, going back to Washington made me believe I could find the beginning again and that might lead to the middle, then perhaps to the end. Not the ultimate. But the end of the horrible events that have plagued our country—the end of this thing that has so wrapped its tentacles around us inside that we can find no way to expel. Every now and then there comes out a trickle of bile. Slowly, we must cleanse ourselves, inside. We must expel the filth.

Wake up, darlings—there's nothing to wait on. You've got to really live it now. The lies, the acting, will not suffice. We're going to have to live it. Who brought us to this? Accuse all you like. But when each one points the finger, make sure it's pointed to yourself, to thine own bosom. And jab hard so you can feel the recognition of self. And do not pity thyself. Only say, "I'm ready to do something about this." And now. Wait no longer for thy neighbor, because with the current crime rate your neighbor may lie murdered in his bed when you go over to knock on his door.

The people are beginning to whisper, truly frightened, looking for someone to help them find their way. What, dears, are you searching for? Yourself? Yes, that's someone.

When America sits back and sees its leaders led off to jail, and placidly sits in its kitchen and says, "Well, that's how it is," it knows full well that it won't be long before the crooks will be back. Can't keep them away? The hell you can't.

You put them in office. They have the audacity to demand patience and fortitude from the people they betrayed. No, we reject them but we are not their judge. Leave them to heaven, to another judgment, a final one.

But it's still yourself who needs purging. Washington is a place where most people visit to ask for something, to take something. It is where I spent part of my childhood. Going back, I found myself—someone just like you: sick at heart, sick at stomach. Hurry up, America, and spit.

A LONG TIME AGO

A long time ago God blessed us with a new land with fruits of greatness, where honesty, love, and truth could prevail. But, I now wonder. Was it ever really meant to be ours?

The American Indian didn't give it up: We took it from him. We started saying long ago—like the children with the taffy pull—it's mine, it's mine, all mine. We're reading books now on all our past, what we now base the country on. And what are we finding? Some of the most corrupt, ungodly acts ever committed are there. And we base the country on this. We are getting what we deserve, and at that, it's late coming. For those who shudder and will call "traitor" to these words, I'd like to ask, "How did we get here? What did we do?"

I don't know what you intend to do or say about all this crap we're taking in this country. But I, for one, if I have to move tomorrow, am going to say my piece. And, I'm sure God will provide me a space somewhere on this earth to live. It is His, you know, and I am—woman, artist, wife, mother, that I am—His child.

FOLKS KEEP ASKING

Folks keep asking me why my book is called *Hurry Up, America, and Spit*. Don't we need more words of praise instead of reviewing what's wrong? Maybe, but recognition of the uglies can open up a sequel, a new beginning. As I travel America, I keep gaining values, increasing knowledge, having thoughts flow in. My wings are stretched widely.

And the learning-tree blooms. My geography and history books come alive, reviving the past, and sometimes they bring hurt and pains. Are we learning from our experiences or merely experiencing, passing our lives?

We have to face the uglies, to admit our errors, and even if we repeat them, we ought not to excuse them. We must rechew our cud—cows in a pasture—and what we cannot live on, or by, we must spit out.

HOW SAD TO BE TOGETHER

How sad to be together—
Alone—together.
Is there such a terrible difference?

A man and a woman are what?
One has to reach out and say,
"Give me understanding,"
"Give me something to feed on."
When one fills inside with silence,
Something is wrong, something is wrong.

Love is taking and giving.
The need of it.
What kind of love is love?
What is the duty of love?
The most necessary thing is love.

To speak, to touch, to hear.
Coming back to that.
They want love forever filled.
But love loses, and never is enough.
I love the sun, yet I cannot keep
Its heat.

~~~~~~

I'd like to look up once or twice a day.
And smile.
And at nightfall, I'd like to look up—
In the moonlight.
And smile.

I might be only a shadow
In each reflection.
But I am myself reflected
In objects of love.

OPENING A CLOSED EYE

Opening a closed eye
America awoke
Turned on the television set
Picked up the newspaper
Tuned in, heard the news
The janitor saw the door free
The building was crept into
The police came
And took men to jail
Someone should help them
Who, who, who
Well, whoever sent him
Well, you should know
You told me
Who told you
Liar you are
I heard it from him.
But you wrote the memo.

Whose duty to whom
Well, call it a favor
Did you warn the chief
Thought you told him
No one should spoil his peace
But he likes peace
Take your orders from me
I'm higher than you
Then it's corruption.
No, a sense of duty only.

~~~~~~

You disobeyed the law
Who disobeyed the law
We are the law
Corruption, no.
A sense of duty only.

Why didn't the man know
I thought he did
Me too
Whose voice runs on that tape
Let me hear it
Well, let him hear it
He did, he heard it.
Why yes, it's okay, I think.

Form the committee
Find out
Just men all just men
Are you peeved Senator?
No more than you Senator.

Inouye seeking to find
Weicker searching and snapping
Gurney smooth as all silk
Thompson drawling back
Montoya reading the lines
Baker asking the question already answered
Erwin playing his old age.

We must not indulge ourselves
In our strengths.
We must get out without fear.
Question, question.
Soon, soon.
Circle, circle.

MAN, I WANT MY IDENTITY

Man, I want my identity—the hue and cry rises. To be known as "a person," anything, but please let me be something. Tell me who I am. Now, how did you get to asking this? Who are your fellowmen? Why are you puzzled? Why don't you know? You are. That's all. Come to grips with this and stop calling to race and creed. *You are.* There. You've just been identified.

Is it a desire for respectability, this being tagged "person" from the day of your conception to your death? Identify with life. If you refuse a man, do it for his sake, not for his group or your group. I want to fight back with this: "Know me, know him." You cannot and will not look below the surface if your eyes are blinded with the mirror of "Who am I?" If the light someday hits that mirror, the reflection will blind you with truth.

Dear God, please close this vicious circle of "Who am I?" and of man seeking not to see himself in all men, of not knowing You are hidden somewhere within us all—in like measure.

ONE, TWO, THREE, O'LARY

One, two, three, o'lary.
Bang goes the gun,
In the schoolyard a child falls dead.
Skip, skip, skip away
To school to learn and play.
Bang goes the gun, a child falls dead.

Teacher, please, may I be excused?
I'm going to the bathroom.
The knife is in the back
Give me your money. No lunch today.

Teacher, Teacher, the young girls ask,
I'd like to go to the bathroom.
Why gone so long?
Panties ripped off
Not long a virgin. She's had it.

Sit down, behave yourself.
Who are you talking to, Teacher?
You. I'm the authority here.
You are? Last month you carried a sign.
Teachers want more pay.
Who's your own authority?

Cigarette? I need a cigarette.
Pass one. Sweet Jesus.
Smoke goes right across the class.
Sweet aroma. Pass it, man.
Tell your man outside the fence.
Bring an ounce tomorrow.

No, man, tell him I can make some
Crazy sales in my algebra class.

Call the School Board.
We must do something about this.
School board meets. Talk.
We need cops in the halls.
We need seats for the incoming students.
Mix them up a bit, that will help.
School's out. The children are out.
How did they escape?
Don't say God in school.
Don't raise that flag up.
Street smarts. Let them learn on the street.

Where did the soldiers come from?
Don't shoot.
Kick or pound the rock.
Bang goes the gun. America goes to school.
School days, rule days.

PHILADELPHIA, PENNSYLVANIA

Philadelphia, Pennsylvania: Ridge Avenue, William Penn High, Reynolds Funeral Parlor (where I last saw Mamma), the fish market, the Pearl Theatre, Central High. Yes, I, too, know Philadelphia. Where did it all go? Where did we let it all go? Another city heading toward decay—sure, there are still beautiful parts—yet the spoils are so general, rottenness is so evident.

Do cities cry? How many times I've waited for trains at North Philadelphia station. Now it's so frightening, you dare not stop. Columbia Avenue, land lying still, people frightened to look left or right as they walk—if they walk. Can a town of decent people reach out and save itself? Can the Liberty Bell be rung again? The mayor, governors, justice department, president, and ourselves search. What's so wrong with other countries that's not so wrong with ourselves?

It's time we made our lives once again our own. Do we waste away our lives to the pace of problems: race problems, school problems, political problems—protest here, strike there—school out, bus in, bus out—the prisons full, the criminals free. The system works, they say. In Philadelphia the Constitution was signed. In the daylight. In the morning. By free men, freely. Wouldn't it be wonderful to walk down the streets of this great old town without looking over your shoulder? Ring that bell, Liberty.

PITTSBURGH, PENNSYLVANIA

Pittsburgh, Pennsylvania: a TV talk-show, speaking on *Hurry Up, America, and Spit.* Somewhere along the line I felt a great urgency, a need for my country to hurry up and cleanse itself before it fell finally ill. "It's not really that drastic," somebody said. Well, if you sit down on your front porch or stand on the corner and watch the appearance of people, the looks on their faces, you would believe exactly what I'm saying. "What are you, Pearl, a pessimist or an optimist?" Neither one. I'm a believer. I believe that where there is sickness there is also health, where there are questions there are also answers, where there is despair there is also hope. A woman wrote me:

Dear Miss Bailey,

After watching you on the "Marie Torre Show" today, I felt inspired to write my thoughts. Your statements concerning our youth were quite correct. I truly fear that if current practices of child-raising are continued, as you so aptly stated, the family unit will fall.

I am an elementary school teacher who has been teaching only a short time, six-and-a-half years. And within that short period, I have noticed much change. In the middle-class community where I teach, it's saddening to see children starved for recognition, concern, and above all, direction from an adult. It's even worse to see adults who are so wrapped up in their own worlds that they cannot recognize or do not want to recognize these children. What happened to the father and mother that took a strong enough interest in their children to supply them with the love and direction which they need? I think the problem is that some do not know what it means to love children anymore.

Suddenly, we have been hit by a number of authorities who are know-alls in child-raising. To them, to love a child is to accept everything that child does as being correct. To tell a child that something is wrong is damaging to his self-image. Listen to him, agree with him, never use negative terms in regard to him, is the trend. For the past two years, I've been approached by parents who tell me that my methods are wrong. I should be completely positive. Address myself only to the things that a child does well. Don't respond to those things that are wrong. I have seen some cases that have disturbed me so greatly that I opened my big mouth, showed anger, and of course, solved nothing. I've seen the father who never told his son that he was wrong. Whatever the son did, or wanted to do, was right. As a result, here is a child, who because he wants only sweets and milk for lunch, is so overweight at the age of ten, that he becomes completely exhausted after climbing the stairs.

I've seen the father who is trying to build a trusting relationship with his son. How? He accepts everything the child says as being true. The others are wrong. Well, here we have an intelli-

~~~~~~

gent boy who now knows that he can do anything and get away with it. That's the exact direction in which he is headed. I have had contact with the parents who do not expect their children to have any kind of responsibility. These children have never been told that what they do is wrong. I could relate many more examples. I should say that parents are not the only people doing this. A number of educators follow the same practice.

To me, this whole attitude of positives is just another way of copping out. Now, don't get me wrong. I am not a negative person. I believe that our youth should know right, and that wrong requires corrective measures. Children need and want discipline. We can't forget that we are dealing with young minds that require guidance and direction in order to develop into strong, sound, adult minds.

My children—and each one that enters my classroom becomes my child even though it's only for nine months (that's all)—are happy, but they are happy because they know that I will support them when they are hurt (physically or emotionally), that I will guide them continuously and teach self-guidance as we go along, and that I am firm in what I say and in what I expect. If they do wrong, they will be told, and they will be disciplined. I have a happy group of children who have not, at least for the short time that they are with me, lost sight of the fact that school is for learning and developing the mind academically and

~~~~~~

socially. We need more people like you who have the respect of the public and can address it as you do trying to make others aware. I applaud you for what you are doing. Please don't stop.

Well, I won't stop, not as long as there are people like this lady calling on me to go on, not as long as that, no sir.

HEADED WHERE?

Headed where?
Wracked with fear and anger
Afraid of truth.
Write it.
Speak it.
Angry voices dissent.
Is it negation?
Pessimistic to accept truth?
Optimistic to accept lies?

Lies entangle.
Opposites no longer attract
And we bend
With confusion.
Avoid reality to hurry
To make believe.
Polish the faults
With part-truths.

Man tidies up with courage
Sings loud his praises.
And why not?

Mother, scold me not
Except in love.

Time, teach me.

ARE YOU LONELY, DEAR GOD?

Are you lonely, dear God? Doesn't anyone talk to you anymore? I've heard them speak of the man folks say was your son. Is he still your son? Did he really die? Do you miss him? Has anyone sat to sup or pray or just visit you lately? Is your house a large or small one? Do you have dogs, too? The sun, moon, ocean, people—do you really have dominion over all these? France, America, Germany, India, Greece, the Middle East—you mean, this territory which men claim is yours? Do you own them outright, or are there debts? How come you're so lonely? I still love you, and every time I run into someone who asks about you, you know what I do? I tell of my love for you. You don't mind, do you? Some just nod. I don't think they've really forgotten you. It's just they stay so busy doing what you've already done—you know how it is. Is that the right way, God? I'll write again real soon. Please keep in touch.

Love,
Pearl

Pearl Bailey

I STAND IN AWE OF NATURE

I stand in awe of nature. I'd like to get hold of twenty-seven federal grants to send some boys and girls and men and women to see the Grand Canyon. Just to stand there and meditate—without a camera in the lot!

Folks who snap picture after picture of one another eliminate this majestice spread from their lenses! Once when I was there, a group went berserk trying to get a snapshot of me. "You don't want me in your picture," I said to them. "It would be an honor," one of them explained to me. "No, no," I had to answer, "what you want to take home with you is the memory of the splendor of this place. Here you can come awake, your senses can come alive, your imagination soars, and you can't help but feel grandeur." I wanted to be friendly. I wanted to touch these people as much as they wanted to touch me. One fragment of a thought kept burning: God, the invisible is made visible. I asked myself, "Did I ever see Him more clearly?"

When I left the mystery of the Grand Canyon, I didn't need a snapshot. I'll recognize it forever. What it represents to me is in every face I see.

I'M PART OF THE WORLD

I'm part of the world, and I happen to live in one
of the greatest countries in the world. Many men
would say THE greatest country in the world. I
use the word ONE because each thing that God
gave us is good and there's no contest: we're a
part of the greatness. I've lived more than half
a century in America and I feel that what I lived
in my childhood, what I saw in my childhood,
certainly wasn't right in this country, nor was it
all wrong. Strange that at this age I can say the
same thing as I could at five- or six-years-old.

A certain deterioration is coming on. Things
we're losing that must be repaired, mended by
loving and caring. Most people in America do
care, do love our country. Yet, in the fast pace of
history, we've lost something of the spirit. Because politicians got lost, we think God did, too.
If this does not destroy the country, it will destroy
the love the people have, and nothing exists without love. We know what we have to do. We can
restore by loving, by caring, by reliving with other
people. We Americans can be good at that. Not
always the best, but good. There's no contest—
except in ourselves.

MANY YEARS WE HAD AMBITIONS

Many years we had ambitions to dig a well for water, to graze the sheep, to thread our looms, to churn our butter. Families did this. Then it came to the point when it wasn't as simple (or as hard) as that for most people. Throughout the history of our country, we opened many frontiers and left them behind us—raw.

Once I was riding along in a certain city, and I looked out the window of the cab. I saw boarded-up houses and people lying in the street. I went through different neighborhoods, seeing different groups, and the scene started to change. It was the change from ghetto to suburb, the ghetto residents become maid and garbageman once they go to the suburbs part-time. Suddenly, I thought, "Why is every man leaving his own house to clean up somebody else's when each man needs to clean his own?" Each person in America today could be free for himself. You agree with that? Then let him have a house of his choosing, where he chooses, and see.

I SENSE GOOD THINGS STIRRING

I sense good things stirring. Maybe it has something to do with the economic situation, but whatever the reason, the change is a delight. Ladies buying yarns and embroidery and patchwork materials, staying home at night. Men cooking. Young couples building furniture, making art. Creative clothes are the rage. Could we be learning again?

I only hope it's not too late. Families are trying to be less strange to each other, keeping together instead of losing one another in having too much. Is there really a crisis? Too bad we can't remain together when the country's in good shape and there is no crisis. Does it take the bad to make the good? Well, yes, sometimes.

WATCHING THE WONDROUS

Watching the wondrous from
The sixteenth floor of the Fairmont
The city squared below.
And across the bay, The Rock.
Alcatraz.
Years of looking out and looking in.
The Indians moved in and out.
A jail, a haven.
Another look and it's not found
In the San Francisco fog.

Men live with fogs between.

MANY MEN SAY I LOVE YOU

Many men say I love you.

Years ago we arrived
At the house of loneliness.
We went in
And love was lonely.
We stayed awhile.
Suddenly we were no longer lonely.
Love grew there.

We had loved,
We had touched love.
Loneliness was no place around.
There was awareness,
A crowded happiness.

Listening always at the door
For the entrance of love.
Coming in, going out.

Be happy, dare to be loving.

YOU KNOW I KNOW YOU

You know I know you.
That's good.
You know it.
Just turn around sometimes in the day
And see askance
Not a word, just a glance.

It will live.
One feels love across the space
And love takes strangeness away.

When there is talk
Someone says your name.
How warm,
How secretly warm.

Do you know what I'm saying?
I love you.

I WAS ASKED

I was asked to go to Washington to speak to a convention for the handicapped. A large man was seated next to me. A friend brought him onto the plane in his arms, literally. He had a big broad smile—going to the convention. What a giant he would have been, standing tall. Somehow, I felt that because of his inner strength he was a giant, sitting. We were both (it turned out) on our way to see four-thousand handicapped people. I was to be one of the speakers. Fairly bursting with anxiety—Oh! I've spoken at schools, but nothing before like this. At the kitchen table, at home, my speech was written from my heart and the top of my head. I was fearful now not to let the right words stray.

The lobby was life in all measures: smiles, greetings, hugs, kisses from people with no arms, no legs, with only one eye, from people with half-bodies. Friendly voices trying to say "Pearl" were mere sounds—grunts, really—but I heard them. A man without one part of his body was helping a friend who had another part missing: They made up for each other.

How do you speak of all this? Man asks, "May I?" God answers, "Yes, you may." Who are the handicapped ones? Are we the handicapped? Hospitals, theaters, all the facilities for living must be opened to these people who are alive.

We're looking at our possible-selves when we see the handicapped ones. Some of us come here, come to life, that way. Many of us are fully crippled, with full capacities to hate.

I went away thinking that, in this present time, instead of passing arms abroad, let us start at home. These hospitals and other places where people live must be kept fresh with ideas and caring. Each of us must do, if we are to survive. If one human being has to stand back because he has been struck a blow, another human cannot undo that person's right to exist fully in this world.

The world needs people. No one can say, in truth, "no one can use you." Not use you? You are needed!

What does it mean, "handicapped"? Break it down. I think of "capped" as having a cap placed on your head—your great attitude toward living. The only handicap any man can have is if God Himself deserts him. This was my first time to meet four-thousand people, a crowd and a gathering of people whose minds and spirits were concentrating on being whole. I realized then I had been handicapped because I hadn't met them before.

I remember what I wrote once before: I've been against the wall, bracing myself, and then quite abruptly, I've taken away the braces, mentally and physically. The braces I didn't need anymore. The wall was standing by itself. It's only you that's leaning. The wall is always straight. It's like the Great Wall of China, going around more than a city. And then one day you'll grow and say, "I always thought there was a wall here, but, you know, there never was a real wall. I imagined it."

MIAMI, MIAMI, MIAMI

Miami, miami, miami
Palm trees, ripened.
On the balcony
Watching the darkness.
White caps rushing in.

Straining to see
God's majesty.

Staring too long, imagining
Big nothingness.

The useless desire.
A thing beyond our grasp.
Lost on the shore.
Lost in the sea.

THE LIGHTS WERE UP

The lights were up. The grunts and groans grew very loud, emotions were running high. The excitement of the show was tearing someone apart.

Someone told me we had guests, but did they really carry on like that? The show ended—lights up. Let's introduce our friends, and there they were. Ten-strong, all in wheelchairs, twisted, mouths opened wide trying so hard to say the words of love and happiness. I left the stage running up the aisle—how unethical in the legitimate theater—and we hugged. We almost choked each other. The people stood, looked, cried. The cast, standing behind me, cried.

Then our guests came backstage. How they carried on! They gave me a present, a multicolored doormat made by themselves. One girl could use only her feet to weave. Some of the grown-ups close by cried and walked away—truthfully, I wonder if I too wanted to go. I stayed. The hospital volunteers stayed—most of them were young people. They kept laughing, talking to them, our guests.

When they received my *Duey* books they went absolutely wild. The girl who used only her feet stretched one foot suddenly, wildly, becoming very upset. All were trying to get her message. "No, no." Her utterances grew louder, and one could see frustration on that face. With a startling flash of insight, I sensed she wanted her name, Ann, in the book, and upon her realization that I knew this, she grew frantic with joy.

Later, the others and I talked about their having to walk away from the pain and strangeness,
and how the children volunteers could stay on,
laughing and talking. Is it because the young of
today are less emotional? Or stronger in love? Is
it because our generation of older people become
frightened by emotion that we run? Or does our
hurt go deeper? Is it that years ago we lived with
cerebral palsy on every block and thought these
people were queer or just unlucky? I don't know.
But I think the young ones are more open to love,
standing there, facing it all. Maybe our children,
yours and mine, are volunteering for the human
race.

I TOOK A TRIP

I took a trip on a train and thought about the mountains looking over the unoccupied plains, silent brooks running through crevices of earth, tumbleweeds pausing in troupes, snow lying in wait on the mountainside to slip into the dry streams, black lava of the past belched from the earth, evergreens standing on the heights, and below—the dirty, scattered huts, some occupied, most not.

The occupants were either too poor or too weak to move on, the finality of life had caught up with them. Little Indian children huddled in the dirt, waiting for a friendly wave, or a curious look from the window of our passing train.

Unrepaired tracks fairly shook the train from its route, tossing and tumbling me in my berth. You could once see America from a train. The good and the bad, the majestic and the low. But the trains are fewer and fewer, shunted, gone. No new ideas improve this great American tradition. The train attendants seem lost, holding memories if they're old enough. Unions put a price on how much one had to tip the porter, the cheapies no less than those who gave decently. Then came the racial issues. Who was a porter? Who was not? There were railroad stations where men carried your bags, tipped their hats, smiled, and were not of your race. Values get mixed up in our great progressive moves. Stations dropping from dozens of porters to five or six, and those miserable self-service carts. Hooray for great ideas. Of course, at the same time, there are people in power thinking how to put men to work.

More people should ride trains. So many children have never had the thrill of getting a first-hand look at this magnificent country. Let's spread the rails—perhaps someone might get an idea how to get people to come out of those crowded ghettos into the open spaces. The tracks could lead. And the children standing by the road, waving at the old dreams, will maybe make it feel all new—to those moving and to those standing still, travelers in time.

HEY YOU OUT THERE

Hey you out there, I remember when we dug in the dirt, walked in the dark, ate in shifts because we had to wait—there wasn't enough to go around. But we got through it.

Involved. *We don't care to get involved.* Isn't it funny, we actually say "care." Where does the period go—at the end of "care," or at the end of "involved"? Years ago, neighbors would go next door, close your window if it rained, watch your children if they knew you were at work, turn down the flame under your pot on your stove. Involvement, doesn't involvement really mean "care"? Are you really saying you don't care? Stop to think, "Oh, God, maybe it could have been me."

Cry, yes. Clean the streets, unboard the buildings—let's hear the heartbeats of people. Come out and look at every man who looks at you. Be a mirror to every man: There is no simpler truth than this. We can get through it with simple truths.

Sure, I'm preaching to myself, but your own self is the beginning even if not the end.

THERE'S A WAY

There's a way to look at the past. I've reached an age when I think more and more of the good in the past. I hardly remember the bad anymore. Is it poor memory? No. All my life I have been able to remember. Lately, I find that I'm not telling the past the way I used to. In events of unpleasantness, I don't see myself as having been a part of it. I know I was there physically, but spiritually I think that I was not. How do I know? Well, the bad events don't govern my conduct now, and they are not repeated at will or by accident.

All of us get caught in the traps of lost love and miserable misunderstanding. But even if that can't be helped, you can still avoid making a pattern out of your bad times. When something unpleasant begins to look familiar to you, move on. I already know my faults. I needn't see them again, in the present or in my memory. There's a way to look at the past. Don't hide from it. It will not catch you if you don't repeat it.

DO THE YOUNG SEEK

Do the young seek absolute truth? Take me along, too. After all, I might have earlier crossed this way, and when you feel as quicksand, I might feel as concrete, the path hardened by values I learned when I passed before.

OPERA, ROCK, AND PLAY

Opera, rock, and play theatergoers are not teased in the clever way these days that moviegoers are. Movies still feature the *chase*, the *battle*, the *shooting*—blood spilling all over the screen.

But it's not innocent as it once was—Indians biting the dust, pirates swept from the deck, soldiers falling from the ranks. In Act One, or better yet, Scene One, before you can sit down, the actors are in bed, caressing, moaning, groaning in what is unintelligible expression. (There are a million ways people can express themselves in tone, with firmness but without vulgarity, but that does not pay at the box office.) The picture opens, the title comes on, a character is seduced, a gun goes off, and half the actors don't have to return for the next day's work.

Next, the ratings. Love the ratings. G, PG, R, and X. G is General. Thank heavens for Walt Disney, dead or alive. PG—Parental Guidance. One day I went to the movies with four little girls— each about twelve—I didn't know it was PG, and when I saw the billing, said to the cashier, "I'm sorry. What's playing next door? I don't intend to go in." "It's all right," she said. "PG means as long as the parent brings them it's okay." I went in because I thought parental guidance was a good thing. (Frankly, I needed someone there with me.) T'was sad watching four little girls trying to giggle without my seeing them. They could have laughed out loud, because I was already in hysterics for being stupid enough to believe PG meant anything.

I'm an actress. I worry about audiences, the four little girls and their misguided adult (me), and all the others. But I worry about actors, too. To make a living, do they have to make out on the screen? One does not have to write the truth with a dictionary of filth. Great stories have been told with style without the shock of the obvious. There's a very powerful English play called *Equus*. As I watched it unfold, I sensed what was happening. The actors disrobed. It was so beautiful, so natural, so necessary to the sense of the play that if they had not done it, it would have been a lie. That's how nudity, and physical love, and even human deformity should be presented: When it is pertinent and true to the artistic intention of the people who act and are directed. When you go to the movies, you shouldn't be *buying sex*. For buying sex—legal or illegal, moral or immoral, reversible or inevitable—should be a *private* act.

YOU CALL YOURSELF WHAT YOU MUST

You call yourself what you must. I don't call myself religious. Other people, I know, call me religious. It's never more than five or six sentences
into an interview before I'm asked, "You're a very
religious person, aren't you?" Is it because I men-
tion God? No, not that alone. Some people men-
tion God in blasphemy, in fright, in menace. His
name is used and misused and made absurd, and
it's not even always the same name. Arthur Clarke
wrote a book called *The Nine Billion Names of
God*. At least.

I'm religious if it means I am aware of my life.
I know that I can't go on singing and performing
forever. One day I will die. I know that God writes
the opening and closing dates on this engagement,
but in the time He gives me I must do as much as
I can, every breathing moment after moment.
What will happen to me when I can't perform?
Then I will do something else as well as I can. It
seems to me that if you stay aware, you open yourself to possibilities.

I didn't write a book until I was in my late
forties, and now I've written five. I didn't travel
abroad just to see and understand the world until
the 1970's, and in mid-decade I became officially
part of the United States Delegation to the United
Nations. What's next? I do not know. Maybe nothing new, and maybe nothing old again.

I have been close with my illnesses, very close.
One day I guess I will get that big pain and a man
will lean over me, and I won't hear him. But then

I'll be safe from harm, and safe from harming others, because then I'll be in the presence of the Creator, whose names are the names of all creation. And if there's something new for me to do then, I suppose He'll tell me.

You call yourself what you must. I don't call myself religious, but I certainly am proud that someone else calls me that.

A LONG TIME AGO,
BUT NOT BEYOND MEMORY   *Ben*

A long time ago, but not beyond memory, the slaves were brought to America. The hurt went deep. Terrible things happened—scars were branded on their bodies and *minds*, and so, maybe marked forever, were their souls. The hurt got even deeper when the slaves' desire to live, to be fully human, became very large, made them fight back. The coming back to manhood for the black man was as terrible as anything he had ever lived under, but he kept at it, struggling for his right to live.

Some men akin to those who beat and tore their flesh stood beside them and said, "We feel your hurt." Sad, the guilt of our own kind seems heavier than any burden that God himself can put upon us. Many white people stood beside us, and with us, and around us, deploring these lashes of cruelty, sometimes shielding us, sometimes turning away in shame.

Do we speak of the "colored race," "the Negro race," "the black race"? What shall we say? Let's call it the race of people with the beautiful skin, the skin that shone under God's sun so long that it turned so very black. It's the race that is like all others in its diversity, in its weakness, in its joy. It's the race of humankind.

You know, the question (and the answer) is not one of race. Maybe nobody knows who nobody is no more. People are beginning to stare at the oddities among us all. Identities are becoming unidentifiable. Those of us who were once outside, are now in. Inside the circle where we of the black race now stand, we should invite our neighbors to come in with us. Some say, "No, none in but us." But if you stay in, maybe you can't get out. When one gets into a maze, it's a very hard thing to get out unless one knows the turnings. We knew the turnings once.

The "race of the Sun" was proud, clean, well-mannered, neat. They had a dignity even in poverty, a way to toss their heads, a beauty that men of other races truly envied. Shall we seek ugliness, or shall we stay in that sun and shine brightly? I make my choice. I hate no one for what he was born. I love everyone for what he may be.

I HEARD FROM A LADY

I heard from a lady named Sally Anderson. She's a nurse who wrote to me on April 4, 1973, and said her letter had to do with truth-marching. She knew a lot of people were demonstrating these days, and she wanted to say that . . . "five years have passed since the killing of Martin Luther King. Have the people chosen to exemplify his ideals by naming a park, a school, a building after him, or forget the man? What did I learn from the '60's? We reached a time when I was able to activate some of the thoughts that had thus far been burned in my head. At last I began to get into the real world. The world where nonwhite people don't have it easy, or even fair and just, in America. The world where national leaders are forceful and vibrant one moment and are mourned the next. The world where civil rights won't exist without first the deaths of *Goodman, Chaney, Schwerner, and poor little girls in Sunday school.* The world where the real meaning of 'Hell no, we won't go!' means jail, or goodbye U.S.A. Forever the world where too many have too much too soon and decide that the only thing left to do is to cop out.

"Despite all this I believe good things are happening. The world is closer together and heads and souls are opening wider and in greater directions than ever before. I believe more people are asking, 'What can we do for our country?' not 'What can our country do for us?' More people are dreaming new dreams of new possibilities and

~~~~~~

saying, 'Why not!' More people are making the dream of freedom a reality. Freedom singing from every mountaintop, every town, every city. Freedom ringing from the depths of every human being.

"We are moving in the right direction to get to the mountaintop to say, 'Free at last! free at last! thank God almighty, we are free at last!'"

I thank you, Sally, for feeling, for speaking. I feel stronger knowing you are a believer in the free choices of free men. I asked Sally, afterward, to write a verse, and so she did. Here it is:

Right on Time

Who knows what will happen any time in our
    lives?
        Sometimes things go on with
        no reason or rhyme.
Something greater and stronger than I makes
    things happen right on time.

Look around every tree and under every stone—
    look up, down, all around and soon you will see
    there is.
Something bigger than all mankind makes the
    right thing happen at just the right time.

BEYOND THE RIVER JORDAN

Beyond the river Jordan, in Amman, I thought: A person thinks that he is the only one in the world who suffers in the moment of his suffering.

Today, I saw a young man with a disease that I've seen often in my country. We've fought, and although we are still fighting a heavy battle against it, we have largely won. Polio.

It was a bright, sunny day. Sitting on the balcony of the Intercontinental Hotel in Amman, Jordan, I saw courage. So I walked down to the pool to watch closer. The youngster on the diving board had a withered leg; his companion, waiting to make the spring, was a plump, well-formed boy. The little handicapped fellow stood flexing his chest muscles as if he were Tarzan. Then he limped very fast to the end of the board and into the pool with a splash. He came up looking proud and when he swam alongside his friend, you could tell that he *knew* they were equal to one another.

A handicap is a state of mind. A disability is a state of body. I went back to my room thinking that if I suffer plainly I must know that there are many people who suffer disabilities, but if I suffer in self-pity, it's because I have handicapped my mind.

PEOPLE IN THE THEATER

People in the theater become involved in politics, and it does not reduce their talent. Many years ago, my thinking on speaking out politically was simply that it was none of the audience's business whom I voted for. It's still my view—in a different sense.

We lived, in our industry, during the frightened age, during the Joe McCarthy period. Thank God, we are no longer governed by the fear that someone won't hire us because of our politics. Maybe the change came about because the biggest thing in the world today is fame—politicians are new celebrities. Wherever you go, it's celebrity that gets attention. Not just in the theater. In politics, surely, and maybe even in literature.

The knowledge of people in the theater applied in right places is invaluable. Remember, our hands are forever on humans—talking with, living with, entertaining them, learning from them. We grow in a mixed garden, all watered-down with the humanness of what we see and hear. We're touched by people—high-life, low-life. People cry out their woes and pleasures to us.

Politician, Citizen: You want us to keep our hands out of politics? Well, just try to do your politicking sitting at your hundred-dollar-plate dinner with no entertaining! A grand lady in politics said to me many years ago, "Oh, my! you're Pearl Bailey. We're having a party at my house and I would ask you to come, but we don't have a piano." I looked at this intelligent lady who sat in

a large governmental position, so pompous, looking down her large elegant nose, and answered,
"It's very good you don't have a piano, because if
you had one, I really wouldn't come."

That was what was for a long time—the artist's *use* to politics. Many people think—numb-
skulls who think the stage is as far as artists reach
—that theatrical people should be apolitical. Who
longs for an audience more than a politician?
Artists know audiences, their strengths and their
weaknesses. They know when tricks are used to
gain attention. They know when feeling is real in
a group. It doesn't make of theater people political
scientists, but it doesn't disqualify them, either. In
the end, it's ideas that prevail. And I see no reason
to accept that being on the stage disqualifies someone from having, or holding, ideas.

WE LOOK INTO MIRRORS

We look into mirrors but we only see the effects of our times on us—not our effect on others. We are becoming the greatest excuse-makers in the world. We even excuse war. Absently, we stare into the present—excusing, forgetting, seldom forgiving, and running from true common sense.

Most Americans know what is right, what is wrong, in this country. As people, we must retain our individuality long enough to recognize our place in this world—knowing that each person is a contributor to some factor of life, knowing that the person you see in the mirror is an actor, not just a victim, in the world.

THE BROWN BOY SAT

The brown boy sat on the sidewalk, comb stuck in the side of his hair. His hair wasn't combed: It just had a comb in it. His friend had no comb in his hair, nor had his hair been graced by one for some time, it appeared. Casually, they leaned against the building, looking down, looking neither left nor right nor up. Once in a while, on the sidewalk outside the drugstore on the main street, one of them would stare at the crowd going by.

We allow this to happen. No, I'm wrong. We do not allow it to happen, but sometimes they get away with it. Leaning, stalling, not going anywhere. What information can be going through these glazed eyes to these lost minds? I'm not too sure they are aware of anything.

What's to be done for these helpless lost children? They do not appear to be on the verge of going in to rob the store nor raping nor mugging anyone—despite the fears of adults who mistake idleness for criminality. They are just there, merely there. Is the world to pass by these lost babes? Somewhere in these hearts, I'm sure, there beats a will to do. If only somewhere, somebody would reach that desire. If only somewhere, somebody paid some attention.

I stopped—and looked—and said a quiet prayer. In my way, I cared, whether they were aware I did or did not. It is not important now, because I did not reach them. Or did I?

RECESS, RECESS

Recess, recess.
Ten minutes for children,
Ten days for Congress.
What can you do in ten minutes?
What can you do in ten days?
Well, it's Easter time.
Chase the bunny.

At odds, the President
With the Congress.
At odds, the Congress
With the President.
The answer: Recess, recess.

People foundering
Petty piddling
Leaders jaunting
Recess, recess.

When they return
They will debate.
Form, reform, form again
Blah-blah-blah.
Recess, recess
Congress recesses
In a recession.
If Congress depresses
Is it a depression?
When they campaign
They take no time off.
Keep them home.
Final recess.

A NATION MUST TAKE PRIDE

A nation must take pride in itself. Any good house-keeper will tell you, it isn't enough to have a clean parlor if you have a filthy kitchen. There is no price for pride. One weeps waiting for humanity to accept humanity—it's the only way.

When our shores were open, people poured through our wide doors. We should never close doors again: School doors, church doors, hospital doors. The fulfillment of that is the survival of our nation. Every man must give a damn about every other man.

Involvement or interference? The world grows smaller, it's said, as we involve ourselves in the affairs of other countries. But I don't believe that. It grows more distant. If the entire world is our burden, then we burden the world with the pace of our ideas, sometimes against the acceptance of other people, and we then grow uncertain or resentful. It's hard to play football with the world, so to speak, huddling, turning, pounding, trying to reach the goal. When the quarterback lets the ball fly, has he picked an honest receiver? Or one who will grab the ball and run toward an opposite goal? We've got to make sure of our direction always.

We've got to show the world our openness in new ways. From other nations students, technicians, and scientists come to us—working at any menial job to learn the American way of making things, of processing information. We should spend time doing the same in their countries—

not for six weeks, but for years at a time, as they do. You cannot be open only if you stay at home. If we take pride in ourselves—if we keep a clean kitchen as well as a clean parlor—then we ought to go abroad to learn as well as to teach. The world is still a very big place. There are things we know for certain. But there are things we have not dreamt of. Shakespeare said it in *Hamlet*. It's still true.

FIGHTING FOR GUN CONTROL

Fighting for gun-control laws seems to be a total loss.

We need weapons only to hunt beasts of the field. Who are these beasts? Humans being mowed down in the streets with carbines? Is America itself becoming a beast? Huge arsenals float in every city and town—within organizations—not hunting clubs.

I stayed at a hotel where the gift shop sold a squirt weapon to put in your purse for protection. I loathed that, but then, when I was about to enter the elevator, two men—looking ferocious—beckoned me to get in. Then, almost, I wished I'd bought the thing in the shop. I am ashamed of that wish, but I could not deny the fear that prompted it.

No count can be made of guns loosed on humanity. The exciting number is the "Saturday Night Special" which doesn't do too bad on *Monday, Tuesday, Wednesday, Thursday,* or *Friday,* either. The lobbyists do not say we must have these guns. No, they argue that laws against weapons will eventually repress all or most guns. They are right: Good laws will make a person prove his need for a gun. "The Indian never kills except when he needs food." What does the modern American need his gun for?

LET ME INTRODUCE YOU

Let me introduce you to a man. He stood tall and sure. He talked of his guitar, of the songs of his people, even promising to translate a song into English. I left him in the store where we met, going back to the car. My children wanted to meet this fascinating man, but he had disappeared. We felt a moment of panic—a feeling of a friend lost!

Then I saw him at the foot of the hill, moving toward his camper. He glided on, as if ahead of the wind, and he turned his elegant head. The children and I raced down the hill to meet him. A woman beat us to him, her arms around him. Soon, at a picnic table we all sat, and my children and I drank the passionate words of his people, their plight and their hope. He sang not in sadness, but in enlightenment.

Our parting was filled with love. As we reached the car, he caught up with us, swift as an eagle. He tied a feather to the car. Suddenly, thunder and lightning flashed, and his dark, beautiful eyes turned to the heavens. He spoke of his respect for thunder. And when I asked him about his eagle feature, he said he had an inheritance of twelve feathers from his grandfather. The eagle, he said, can fly directly into the sun. Lightly, I touched his arms. He never quivered, he never moved—it was as if the gesture were permissible, yet forbidden.

I silently thanked God for showing us the spirit of this Winnebago Indian. He gave us so much. Surely, we'll meet again in some deep gorge, he a human being who had been pushed into

~~~~~~

darkness by the latest and perhaps the last Americans. They who worshiped the light were shoved into darkness. Now they must be brought out once again in the stream of living within their own country. They once moved pretty far from us— from the shores where they watched our arrival, away to the forest and hills. But we drove them farther, deeper still, so far that most of us have never seen them and do not know them.

RIDING ALONG THE RAILS

Riding along the rails toward the land of dogwood
and magnolias, I thought of prejudice, of hatred
long bathed in blood. I thought of men deciding
to free themselves from their own country's law-
ful tyrannies. Men wanting to sit, walk, talk, at
will. Are we still paying the price, which has become very high? Some hatreds vanished and good
things grew, but many things have grown worse.
Slogans pop up from all sides and some of them
create ugly moments.

The fear we live with now is a progression—
from where? Some mistakes of the past are being
slowly rectified—not all of them, not by all of us.
Where the blacks have found a chance for prog-
ress, they have progressed. Where there were no
waves, they strove to make some. The world be-
lieved that only a certain section of our country
cast atrocities. Not the North, not the West. Oh
Lawdy, not the East where the "liberals" are getting more unbearable to each other every day—
they are losing the human element. It's frightening that in the year 1976, celebrating a victory of
freedom, we still are trying to free people of the
inequities of "materialism." God!

What holds the South together is that Southerners had to take long hard looks at themselves
in the mirror of history. We all still can do that.
What do you see? We must change in order to
survive. The South found it out at a terrible price
to itself—they were embarrassed by reaction, os-
tracized by belief. Yet I choose to think that the

Southerners finally did try to cleanse themselves. There's a feeling of patience and courtesy in the South that cannot be ascribed to the old-time wary black man alone. It belongs to the white man, too. I wish, oh, how I wish, I found it in the "liberal" societies elsewhere in our country.

IT WAS A LOVELY DAY

It was a lovely day. I decided to take a stroll, but not too long a walk—that can be a little dangerous in America today. I wanted to enjoy the beautiful park, look at some of the exciting new buildings. This was New York City with *unoccupied* new buildings. What's that all about, I thought? Why spoil a good walk? Meditate on the good. Okay.

On the corner, waiting for the traffic light to change, I was enjoying all the sights and sounds, the people passing. Suddenly, I had the queerest feeling: Parts of me were missing—someone had taken something from me. *My backside.* In the hands of a man behind me. *Both of his hands.* The fury I felt was no match for his anger. I demanded he release my private property and he screamed, "I'm showing you I have no prejudice." Controlled, I asked him, "Do you have to do it this way?" He continued to indulge his urge to possess my private property. I got him to release his hands.

The people around us became an audience as they stood gawking, waiting to hear the outcome. Two policemen walked on the other side of the street. "Officers," I yelled and they came, but not too fast. The incident was explained. I was invited to come to the station to lodge a complaint. Meanwhile, my friend was screaming that his desire was to "save race hatred." Finally, he was so disgusted with the whole scene, with the officers telling him that he was wrong (and, maybe, with my own decision not to go to the station house), that he decided to make a citizen's arrest of *me*.

In sheer disgust, the policemen and I all turned away.

The moral is, if you ever decide to go for a walk in the good new liberated days in America, "Watch Your Ass."

MOSES, MOHAMMED

Moses, Mohammed, the Twelve Tribes of Israel, Ali Baba and the Forty Thieves, Pharaoh, the Sphinx, Jerusalem—after all, these are familiar names, but how much do we really know about the Middle East?

There are strange roots in that part of the world, in a nurtured earth, rich of oil, poor of other things. People move in flowing robes of spun cotton, some in rags, beautiful people all browned by the sun, multicolored people.

There are mosques and temples made of ceramic, turquoise, and gold. There are mud huts like hives where children, mules, old people, and flies are crowded. Women walk with babies sucking at the tit, hiding the fact there's no other food —as the rich ride by. Fires burning low, pots hung high—everyone huddled around, waiting, waiting. Soon there will come the bowl and the dip of goodness.

Meetings in circles. "Where do we go from here?" I hope that the people who talk and ask will keep in mind, seared in mind, the people in those huts who sit and wait.

SITTING IN LAFAYETTE PARK

Sitting in Lafayette Park, across from the Hay Adams in Washington, D.C., I thought, "What a beautiful day to walk and meditate." As I strolled and looked at the orangy-red tulips beginning to unfold (the cold winds had made them keep their coats longer than usual) in the warmth of the sun. A mass of men were walking, discussing, and standing by the tall picket fence in front of the White House. Not unusual. People are always protesting and pleading (or listening) outside that big, white house. There are people doing the same inside. I've been there. I can say it.

Policemen were watching the action. The men on one side with their banners were leaning on a rope looking at the policemen. Some were trying to get the attention of cars passing by. Some even sat on the concrete ledge along the fence. All looked lost. You know, it's strange to walk among disturbed humanity. Feeling and living from a distance gives one a different aspect from being up-close. Looking into the eyes of a man, you just might feel his heart.

Two days later, I was in Huntington, West Virginia, the home of some of these men and a city I'd never visited. Outside my hotel, I saw a long string of men who passed me as they went the opposite way. One stopped in recognition. He said, "We are miners." I asked, "Are you the gentlemen that were at the White House last week?" They said, "Yes." They began to tell me about the strip-mining bill. I asked questions. They gave back angry and hurt answers. They explained how they dig down to a certain level, and then pack dirt. They drew pictures and I asked questions. They explained the taking of the earth; they spoke of "shale villages" and "shale golf courses."

"In Washington, they did not even know what we were talking about." Some said they were treated arrogantly in the hotels, though they were clean, because they were miners. They felt lost. I said to them, "Why didn't you wear your lamps on your hats and your workclothes from the mines with the dirt and grime? You'd have been noticed for what you are, for what you want." I wish I could go back to Huntington, West Virginia, put on a miner's lamp, the overalls, and face it. I don't know how deep I could go in that earth.

I'd like to walk along the tunnels under those mountains. I've been inside the White House a lot but I had not been where those miners were, and I feel that I know too little about being inside, which in this case is outside.

THE ROOM LOOKED ENORMOUS

The room looked enormous. Then it shrunk. The man overcame its size. Louis and I sat on the sofa and the man sat in the straight chair on my right. There was another chair there, ready for use, but the man was sufficient company. We spoke of his children, of life, of God; and in all these I think the man, Louis and I, stood equal. He said he was a mystic. Three times he took off his glasses and intently studied me. We said things together as if breathing the same breath.

This went on for about forty-five minutes. He laughed quietly, grew serious. His depth was enormous, his words made sense. Wisdom poured from his eyes. If hostile soldiers were at the door, I wouldn't wonder that he would open it and himself let them in.

Eight weeks later, maybe longer, I saw him again in America. It was past, present, and future meeting, for many years ago Louis and I met him in the woods north of San Francisco. That time, like this one, there was the same serene composure, and underneath a volcano lay.

Recently, he did a fantastic thing. In the middle of Americans' deep, disastrous confusion over oil, he made a speech to the world, discussing the whys and wherefores. Some Americans reared up on their heels, shook their heads, rattled their brains and started to think. This man from afar spoke words so the man in the street could know the truth, loud and clear. Soon the big shots were heard saying that he "meddled." Well, meddling is a word we know a lot about. We know about taking care of our enemies. We even feed them, making their bellies fat so they can stay healthy until they do battle with us. We need friends. We might just need this man. We have needed and *used* quite a few.

Oh, yes, oil is a huge problem. There's a shortage. There always was, there always will be. If certain countries quit sending, we will run low, possibly even run out. Let's guess at some of the nonsense that we accept as excuses now. Oil, like a lot of things, was produced and purveyed and priced under a collaboration of a few large companies and the government. We are a united people, and a great nation. We'll stand behind our government and do with or without. But tell us the truth. We can accept the possibility that this commodity will cost more, that hardships will increase, but don't tell us that the villains are people who are doing with their resources what we have ourselves done.

I think often about the man from Persia's statement, a man we say is our ally, this man who sits among those whom we call our enemies. Unafraid, he remains our friend. From the Shah of Iran, whom I have met with pleasure and reward in the past and present, I learned that each man sees his needs as necessary, and so takes pride in their fulfillment. Do we turn our backs on anyone who tells us things which make us question our leaders? I cannot believe we do for long. We prize

~~~~~~

(it's pride again) our practicality. The Shah knows that we need oil. He knows that we'll not in the end go without energy. He will talk about our living together sensibly because he wants from us what we will sell to obtain from him. His is not a craven nation. Between nations, pride can be honored without too great a price. Is it strange? I learned that from the Shah, not Mr. Simon.

SITTING IN THE CUBBYHOLE

Sitting in the cubbyhole
Not feeling safe.
Come out, join the race.
Let others in the gate
Into your lifeyard.
Open the back door too.
Either way, let them in.

It's good, a front and back door
in case of fire.
The fire of passion,
The fire of hatred,
The fire of love.

THE DOOR CELL LOOKS UGLY

The door cell looks ugly, big black bars closing in humanity. What did that human being do? Did he have a chance to tell what he has done? The jails fill, and then they overfill. There's rioting, breaking out, like movie scenarios: The stench, horror, frustration, the savage togetherness.

Human into savage? Savage into human? What is a savage? When a man commits a proven crime, he should be punished, we all agree. Indecent acts are acts against dignity. If we must punish indecency, we must. The caged need to have a keeper to temper them. But how often now the keeper is worse than the criminal!

It's necessary to judge fairly by trial, but it's also necessary to know the man, in part, by the crime he committed. Men who commit crimes can be categorized. A murderer has killed, a thief has stolen, a rapist has violated a human being. The criminals do not hesitate to categorize themselves, even stereotype themselves. Isn't it strange there's snobbery among all these criminals? The word passes that a certain prisoner is being brought in for a certain crime. Would you believe that the others are offended that he's put among them? Nothing is more distasteful to an embezzler than a child molester who in turn cannot abide an infant beater. The heroin user disdains the rapist.

The just do not consider the *victim* of crime, and they judge the perpetrator only on the event, not on his history. It is not just an overcrowded prison that we must be afraid of. In a world of unclassified criminals every man is a prisoner. Can't we see this? The institution is the world. Laws now are made for criminals more than for the victims. Let us ask what kind of people are victims? What kind of people meet criminals? Often, they are alike.

WHEN I WAS LITTLE

When I was little we played a game—*Run to the East, run to the West, run to the one that you love best.* You ran to the person that you loved the best in the circle, and there'd be laughter. The question now is, whom do we love the best? In this mixed-up world of today, running to the East could mean deadly turmoil and strife and hatred, an entanglement with ambitions of men who hold the products and desires to enlarge themselves. The East. Is this their first chance? To reach out and touch, what? Destruction? Hope? Men with philosophies, dreams, new-found wealth—suddenly they came into their own. As their fortunes grow large, we cringe. The thing that has opened their dream-door slammed the door in our face. We who possessed are now possessed.

Our western world, an overloaded cistern of oil, wheat, corn, necessities, made men rush to us. Our grandeur, made of living blown-up like a great dirigible, made us lose sight of the other balloons in the atmosphere. The shifting of the wind causes a greater need for our knowledge and understanding. Did we think the day would never come? It's here. We must look again to our land. Work our land. Find that underwealth God has provided.

Oil is turning the world topsy-turvy. Certainly, we knew long ago that someday we'd have to meet men who'd figure out what they had. The time is now.

A STRANGE GIRL

A strange girl popped out of a swimming pool, eyes glazed. "He was dead." Now, I was needle-pointing quietly, my thoughts at peace, when I heard this statement. First shock, then amazement, then, "Who is dead?" "The man on the plane," she said. "Dear heart, why are you saying this to me," I asked as she clung to the concrete wall. "I had to tell somebody," she said. Then she swam away. Still awed, I wondered if the sun had not beamed too brightly on my head, but she was back with the same look, same statement. "Swim down to the end, dear. I'll talk to you." She was absolutely out of it. Helping that frightened child out of the water was not easy, tall and strong as she was. On finding out that her parents were upstairs, I called them. She had not answered my request for the room number but handed me her key. All I could say was, "Come get your daughter —she's in shock." Then she said, "They kept drinking on the plane. They should have been praying."

Much later, she wrote me. I've heard from her twice since. She seems still a bit confused, still horribly lonely and lost. I tried to help her to hold to truth. She's inwardly blaming her feelings and, at sixteen-years-old, her lost life. Who is really to blame for our children? Who lost whom? Children or parents?

~~~~~~

Mrs. Bailey,

I must thank you for taking the time to care. I've never met anyone with so much serenity. DeeDee and Candy are fantastic girls and they really showed me a great time last night. I know that you've seen a part of me that I was afraid to show until yesterday.

I'm starting your book The Raw Pearl *today on the plane. Wow! I really wish my parents understood me like you do your girls. I also wish I didn't have to leave.*

May the longtime sun shine upon you,
All love surround you, and the
pure light within you guide you all the way home.
May the Lord bless you,

     Love to all,

I had to smile, think, and yes, cry a little, over her line—"I really wish my parents understood me like you do. . . ." All summer, that time, I was struggling to figure out three girls of her age. We always look stronger to strangers, for it is our own who press us always, looking for weakness while they ask for help.

MEN MINGLE

Men mingle with the others
Who will enhance them.
Crowds pouring in, drinking.
Laughing over their fingers.
Canapes, diamonds large and small.
Entrances observed
These in front, those in the back.
Large checks, small checks.
That dress is a holdover,
The real thing? No, a copy.
Green or blue velvet,
No more blue-suit days.
Everyone waiting for signs,
Fawning, pawning their whispers.
Groups grow and sort,
Multiply, add, subtract.
One olive, two olives, three olives.
Truths emerge and regroup.
Repetition tires.
Tomorrow each will wonder
Whom to tell.
Everyone hangs in,
it all hangs out.

THERE'S A NEW CRISIS

There's a new crisis today. We've got to dim the lights. Electricity is ebbing. How long has it been since we've seen real darkness? In the pre-Edison days we had kerosene lamps, candles, and when electricity was handed us, we went bananas. How brightly all these years our lights have gleamed. Daylight went out of style because the dark was always lighted. This magic thing was used like the sun. We counted on it to infinity. Then came the announcement to "turn down the lights." Power is low. Darkness grew. Fears heightened. We had forgotten the dark and it became strange.

Crisis. It happens to people who allow the plain things to grow strange to them.

I have heard the cries of America from near and afar, from its natives. I've seen with the eyes of others, heard with their ears, touched with their hands. I've watched other people speaking out, fighting back, caring only to strengthen what we all want: our country as the uncle of ourselves. I've watched them and know that America has to spit out its weakness.

In America, we have people who are too rich, people who are too poor, people who are hungry, people who are sick, people who are homeless, people who are imprisoned, people who are bored, people who are strung-out, people who are lonely, people who are exploited, people who lose and can't find their way, people who give up on life. America, we better live as sisters and brothers. Let us take care of our land. We cannot stand up for every other land. Stand up for ourselves.

LOVE FOUND WHEREVER

You know,
I love you.
Hey, that's good!
You *know*.
You turn around
At times
And catch my glance.
Not a word—
Just a glance.
But you know
What you see.
You know I love you.
And I know you love me.

WE'RE FOR SALE

We're for sale, America, and no one cares to buy us. Why don't we repurchase ourselves, pay our debt to ourselves, accept what we have, what we've always had, and mark it paid and final?

THE SOUNDS OF GOODNESS

The sounds of goodness
Where are they gone?
Sounds of wrong ring—
Drum down the senses.
Disaster, disaster,
Do the riots come?
The sun is hot.

Humanity, hand-to-hand
In hopelessness.
Strangers coming my way
Do they hold or seize?
In a land so large
Inside sits the child.
Who mourns? Mother America?

THE ROOM IS FULL

The room is full
The Diplomat has arrived
what country? who cares?
see his suit's sheen?
what color are his eyes?
how did he reach here?
He knew "what's-his-name"
He had "oh-so-much"
The man came from "you-know."
is he learned?
does it count?
He's a Diplomat.
He forms the circle.
did he nod across the room?
making a sale?
a victim or ally?
A set up.

Will he report home?
Not much good; not much bad.
A handshake, a kiss.
Two cheeks, whispers in ears.
The slithering through,
Watching all; confiding none.

Alert to his power
Aware of his limit
These are the same.
Diplomatic, of course.

IT WAS A CHILLY DAY

It was a chilly day; there I was on my way to Jackson, Mississippi—not far from Philadelphia, McComb, and "Old Miss." Yes sir, Jackson, Mississippi. In other places men have shuddered and shivered in fear and hatred and disgust even of its name, Mississippi, M-I-S-S-I-S-S-I-P-P-I.

Once again, I was in the Deep South. I'd been in Alabama, Georgia, Louisiana, but heavens-to-Betsy, not in Mississippi. No sooner did I land, than I was swept off my feet with love. It was unbelievable. Now what to do? We stopped in the coffee shop. I left the windows down, car unlocked, mink coat inside. It was still there, safe after an hour. How exciting and rare!

I strolled to the end of Capital Street, turned, and saw a lady focusing a camera. I made the front page just walking down a main street in Mississippi. There was a time when blacks running down the streets in Mississippi made the news by just trying to survive. But now they came out of stores, waved from windows. Was it just because I was a celebrity? I choose to hope it was because I am a human being.

Press conference at the State Fair. Without ugliness, people were intelligently interested in issues touching on race and belief. Yes, I was still in Mississippi. People, we touched, we laughed—together. I felt safe.

As we practiced, I asked my pianist, "What's new?" He said, "Nothing, not since the robbery this morning." "The robbery?" "Yes, seven people in the hotel were robbed." Oh. That morning my door of the living room was ajar. For sure, my husband had closed it the night before. Well, I thought, the maid must have opened it, and said, "Oops, it's too early." Better count your change, ole girl, I thought. Laughing, hopeful, I felt in my change purse, took one look at the money clip. Aha! $92.00 gone. "E.B.," I said to my friend who travels with me, "call the police at the hotel. I have been robbed."

All day long I'd been drooling over "safety." But now! What about my fur coat? Gone. Well, we were alive. Who knows what the robber thought who looked upon us asleep. Just then, a gentleman, looking very sad, came up to me. "I hope you forgive us for what happened here."

Time passed. I left Jackson, Mississippi. They took something. I took something. Not selfishly, we both gave. Materially, the coat was gone. I could have used the coat, but I needed the love.

ASK NO QUESTIONS

Ask no questions
There could be answers.
What's the end of war?
Do the dead save the living?
The dead do not know.

Men stand on corners
Asking your vote.
I will give you answers,
Send me to the center,
Trust me. Trust me.
Give me no answers.
Promise me questions.

DAILY, ONE WATCHED

Daily, one watched, after Watergate, men of daring deeds, now cringing, fighting back, not remembering, lying. Some were telling truths—but all of them were afraid. Of what? Each other? Yet, when they were so much larger than life, they had fawned, pawed, and stepped on each other. Did they feel pain? There they sat, afraid or ashamed to look at each other. Lawyers with liars and liars with lawyers. Truth-tellers with lawyers and lawyers with truth-tellers.

They might save themselves with all their legal knowledge. But we can save the rest of us by a wary practice of law, day in, day out. There are bad societies which have good laws. That's the irony and the warning.

THE SENSELESS STATIONS

The senseless stations
In our world
Big ones sitting tall,
Little ones below.
Strange. Strange
Where is a middleman?

Are we all, all of us
Lost in the middle?
Caught between
The unremembered past?
The unfigured future?

ARE WE DISPLEASED

Are we displeased with ourselves? Some liberals are all talk and no action. They want credentials more than they want action, I sometimes think. The main streets of the North are becoming more like the backwoods of the South. The North has lived under a thin veil of liberalism.

People in general are not people at all. I know that. There are men and women leading all sorts of crusades today. All of a sudden, there's a lot of leading. That's good. At least, that way we see individuals.

But then, I ask myself: How can I lead my brother down a path when I'm stumbling myself? Someone asked me once on a TV show whether or not I "marched." I said, "No, I haven't marched any place physically, but I live with humanity every day, and when you live with humanity, then you have walked with them—slow as it may be."

People say, "Don't do this. Don't go there. They're using you as they have used Negroes through the years." That is insulting. I cannot represent any single group. And if I am used, it is because I feel I am useful. I'd rather be used, even maliciously now and then, than be inactive.

WHITEHOUSE

~~~~~~~~~~~~~~~~~~~~~~~~~~~~~~~~~~~~~~~

WHITEHOUSE
GOVT WHITE HOUSE DC OCT 28
PMS MISS PEARL BAILEY
SHUBERT THEATRE
BOSTON, MA

THE WHITE HOUSE SPARKLED LAST NIGHT
WITH THAT SPECIAL FEELING ONLY YOU CAN
CONVEY. FOR ONE VERY SHORT HOUR THE
ROOM WAS FILLED WITH LOVE AND GOODWILL.
THE CAUSE OF WORLD PEACE AND FRIENDSHIP
WAS GIVEN ANOTHER SHOT IN THE ARM BY
OUR DEAR AMBASSADOR OF LOVE/

JUST LIKE A GOOD FRIEND YOU WERE THERE
WHEN WE NEEDED YOU. WE WILL NEVER FOR-
GET IT. YOU AND LOUIS ARE TERRIFIC AND A
GREAT TEAM. GOD BLESS YOU BOTH.
GERALD FORD

SEEK TO LIVE

Seek to live.
Looking back
Deadly, not living.
Many men die
Without knowing fear.
In death only
At the last moment
Fear gives way.

A MAN PUNISHED

A man punished sometimes is better than a man imprisoned. The Moslem nations believe that, and to us they seem inhumanly harsh. Sitting in some of the comfortable prisons—there are a few around—suits some men fine. Punishment should suit no one. It should, I think, be brief but intense. Americans will not cut off a man's hand for stealing, I know. But have they considered other means? I ask. I'd like to hear the answer. Wouldn't you?

LONG AGO WE DECIDED

Long ago we decided to help our own. But it got complicated. There were more of us, and some of us didn't belong to anyone. So we created welfare. First, it was a token, then a great organization— one of the most important in our society today. But it began to be well used by many citizens who sit on their fat caucuses, not in truth needing assistance. They're getting fat on their laziness.

Welfare can help. Who will deny it? Persons in poor health, persons who really look for a job and cannot find one, children who need growing up, mothers who need a chance to raise their own. But the critics make it sound a cheat and a fraud.

There's a scarcity of jobs. Jobs are available because they are not sought after. Who will deny it? To participate in the stream of life brings happiness, but we've lost some of the push of life. Why should a person sweat to earn when a like one can go to the mailbox and find the welfare check?

All who are well should be made to seek employment. It's as simple, and as hard, as that. It's not only hard on the workers. It's hard on the managers of our society. For they must be fair in allotting jobs, in making sure that those who are out of luck are not used like migrant workers—we know of that abuse and must guard against greed in managers.

We all know of fellow beings who are offered jobs and say, "I'd love to take it, but I have my animals to care for," or some other crazy reason.

We deserve what we're getting. We pay taxes for welfare. Too much. Let's ask how it's spent. We need tough and fair social workers. Let me tell you about the poor—I know as one who was poor herself. The poor are sometimes cunning because they have to be. They will lie to gain goods. I don't condemn them for that. But I am a realist and know them for that—and that is not their only trait!—and I know that social workers, to be fair, need to be as tough as the poor are. And to be fair, we should not let human beings lie fallow. Equity is as equity does.

A CHILD ASKED

A child asked my husband if people would read what he wrote. The child was in a home, not his own, among strangers. He wanted, he said, his voice to be heard.

The Dandelion

I'm like a dandelion,
All alone,
Free as can be,
Ugly and prone.
Small, as you may see.

Untouched!

Left to die,
I am a dandelion,
That's why I cry.

Yes, Michael Berger, we hear you. And others will hear you, too.

AMERICA GREW TOO FAST

America grew too fast. We Americans ask questions we cannot answer because we skipped something. Maybe it was our childhood. We have lied and lied and lied to ourselves. We cannot lie any longer by telling ourselves that we are all of us free. We cannot send men to fight just wars when they act unjustly, group against group, at home. We cannot tell ourselves that our children play happily if they fear the color of their skins. We cannot tell ourselves that we have a civilized nation when we cannot accept other civilizations. The idea of "separate but equal" is a lie. Separation hurts.

Why do we, suddenly, find the Indian interesting? Some of us adopt the ways of the Indians—wearing moccasins, headbands, and beads. We have discovered the way of the Africans, with high hair, with hair in tight strands; or we see suddenly the way of the early Christians and later Buddhists, with feet bared and with flowing robes. All of this is motivated by something more than fad or chic, even if it has some of that, too.

God created us all. For heaven's sake, accept that. Something larger than ourselves is in our being: In love, we were created.

The hope for political solutions lies in ideas, of course, but it lies in the feeling of wholeness. We don't need new prophets. We need listeners. People who listen and touch and say, "Well, all right, all right."

I AM NAKED

I am naked.
I cannot
Hide from me.
I search
An aim,
A corner.
I want to be
At the end.

A CHILD WROTE A POEM

A child wrote a poem and sent it to me. The essence is one that many people in the audience seem to feel: They get a vision of an actor in the theater and they feel that the privacy of that person is unnatural. You have no private life, you belong to the public. I think the public must educate itself that if you pass them by, it may be that you have to go to work, you have to shop for your house, you have to be on time—it's as simple as that. They often start off their letters with, "I'm sure you'll never see this." How can they be sure of what they don't know? Something like this happened when a child wrote me a letter. I wrote back. Then she wrote me that she shouldn't have written the one she did because it was insulting, and now her dream was alive again because of the answer. But she wanted to be sure that it was I, and not my secretary, who had answered her letter—although it was very plain that it was I. I thanked her for what she had done. When she wrote and explained that she had forgiven me, she said she found me. She was glad again. She wrote a poem about how she felt.

For My Friend

She had magic
I put her in my box.
Nestled her safely between
Unicorns and Pegasuses.

She was cold in my box
Among the fragile magic.
She struggled and pushed
But she didn't know
I had placed the box high.
She fell and shattered.
I was afraid. I wanted to run
Instead I was drawn nearer
To the pieces on the floor.

It weaves a magic, love,
One learns to fondle it.
The edge of a broken love
    is severe.
I keep a box of magic upon
My highest shelf.
But I keep the magic of love,
Inside, inside, inside.
Where I made a friend.

I AM TERRIBLY FRIGHTENED

I am terribly frightened by men who stand ac-
cused and who fear not being right. Perhaps if
they see what in the world is wrong, they might
get it right.

Who judges? Only each of us knows truly what
judgment we deserve: The spectator, the judge,
the lawyer, the indicted, each sits within himself.
Who is true, finally, to himself outside?

I slumped down in the train one day, fatigued,
yet fatigue had not set in the body so much as in
the mind. Gazing out, my thoughts became
strange. Womanhood—past, present, future, all
into one—crowded into my mind. Loneliness is
really soothing. It's breathing new life into me.

I'm coming along, shedding the skin of old.
The crust is hard in spots. Tear the old skin off.
It bleeds a little. I like you as you are, someone
said. But no, let me change, and if it hurts, then
bathe me in the oil of your affection. If I change,
it's because I've judged myself and condemned
myself. And in the light will be the reflection of
what has been, what is, and what must yet be.

THE LIGHT KEPT GOING

The light kept going
On and off in the train.
In the deepened dark,
The shadows of the dark hills
All stuck around.
It's late out there
It's quiet inside.

A man walks beside the train,
One or two or three get on.
In an empty railroad station
Something terriby lonely
And sitting in a train
The train is a stage,
The platform empty seats.
Who can be out there?
Who can be in here?
Turning, hissing, moving on
Somebody left, somebody taken,
A moment missed or not known.

SOMEBODY WROTE ME

Somebody wrote me. "Thank you for loving me
the way humanity should love humanity. That's
all I wanted from you anyway. I've decided to
join the human race. When I read the letter you
sent me, I remembered a poem I memorized a
long time ago. Here it is:

Around the keep of a Southern came the sea,
and the sun looked over the mountain's rim.
And straight was the path of gold for him
and the needs of a world of men for me.

   "I remembered that now. I'll just always love
you, Pearl."

BILL, YOU KNOW

Bill,

You know the title I've always had. While you were away, I got a new one. I think it's terribly important to tell about the fact that I had never been in the UN building. I went on November tenth, for the first time ever, to that building. I felt I was walking into the space of time. I envisioned the many colors, races, and creeds and heard the sounds of all the things I always watched on TV. I don't know why I really had never been there. But at this point in my life, I felt I would like to sit there among men, not as a politician, just as a person who wanted to hear the representation of all the world—the men who spoke for their countries, the men who are supposed to care desperately to keep this great big world together.

So, crossing that concrete walk into the building, I felt I was into something where I felt, quite unexpectedly, I was terribly needed—and I hoped so—and where I could learn and study and achieve. Nobody asked me. But who needs to be asked to give of myself? Michelle was with me— she's all of twenty-four. Well, we got upstairs and we sat at the top part of the gallery and that was the day that they were voting on the resolution condemning Zionism as racism. Well, sir, I put that earphone on and for six hours I didn't miss a speaker—in fact to be very frank, after I got the ingredient of what one man was saying and I could no longer sit, rushed out, and was completely exhausted by the quickness. And all the time I felt like I had done something wrong—which was really to go to the ladies' room. I didn't want to miss one bit of what was said.

One man spoke with passion, another with anger, another with sorrow. I stood in the hall and thought that it was opinion and feeling that distinguished one country from another, not size or importance, for some countries who never would even have thought of being recognized were sitting there in greater numbers than the large powers. How and why have we ever over-looked these small countries? I will not say we overlooked them. We sort of owned them—they were the colonies of the big powers of our world.

All of a sudden, in the room there loomed the smaller nations of the world in great force with voices, wheeling and dealing power. The more the big powers spoke, the more the big powers exer-cised their strength, the more the great powers said, "This will happen and that will not happen" (which a few years back would have scared the pants off everybody), the less they convinced me. I could sense that. They were talking to the air. I don't know why they don't sense it. Probably they do. There were accusations. There were threats. There was misunderstanding. Men said, "I don't know the meaning of the word we are voting on." And they went to dictionaries, and a few times they threw in what the Bible or the Koran said.

All the time, everybody's mind was made up, I am sure. Not one speaker swayed anyone in the hall. One of the most sensible delegates was a man from Fiji. Fiji! How large could Fiji be? And he said what I had for the past six hours wanted to scream from the back of the room. "I don't know," he said, "if all of us in here, which one of us here, which country in here, doesn't practice some form of discrimination." And you know, it should have made normal men think. I just wanted to go up and hug that man. Because here the people were voting on the issue that there should be no form of discrimination against men of race and religion. That's one point.

I listened to some countries that I myself have visited and have seen how they persecuted people, how they practiced great discrimination in all forms, yet here they were defending and pounding for a position they could not uphold at home.

I wondered, later on, when I read that resolution put on the floor to the committees, whether there would be many rallies, with thousands and thousands of people screaming against this resolution. It happened.

Countries are screaming. Enemies and friends have interlocked, allies put together hastily. Yet in that room I wondered who was truly happy. There was a lot of applause. A victory was won. And the minute the applause stopped, there was a feeling within me that you get when you watch a child beaten in the schoolyard. What have we all done? The victor and the victims seemed to have the same thoughts. What have we all done? By then it had been done. The victors and victims of November 10, 1975.

All I know is that my desire is to sit in that building among my fellowmen of all races and all countries where all humanity can be strengthened. Truly I do not know what I can do—maybe nothing. I just would like to sit there and learn and study, and perhaps speak once. And if my speech fails me, then I'd sing a psalm.

I'm speaking of victor and victims. All I know is that in that moment, I felt the passion of hatred and cunning. The one thing I wasn't feeling was love. All the diplomats, everyone, can get all the reasoning and meaning they want in what they said. As a person who sat in that gallery, the hatred that emanated made me sick. I saw victors and victims lose something, but the cause—the thing itself—was not lost. Yes, there is hope. I believe in hope. I believe in not quitting. I believe in love. Peace, Pearl.

HURRY UP, AMERICA

Hurry Up, America, and Spit!

You'll be late for your own show.
You did the hiring, the firing.
Your money is invested here.
Boy, do we love money.
Once, remember, we loved love.

Hurry up and spit.

Spit up, rid yourself.
Settle down, settle up.
You did not start sick.
You didn't find the land spoiled.

Hurry Up, America, and Spit.

Push, America, push.

Look up when you can.
Unlock the doors, America.
You can walk out, not run.
Hold meetings, America.
The rich tell the poor.
The poor tell the rich.
Let the hard words be said.

Bow down, America, and pray.

We are not larger than life.
Oh, my God, help us.

~~~~~~~~~~~~~~~~~~~~~~~~~~~~~~~~~~~~~~~

Where did it all go?
Our lot, our own, our pride?
It's not lost, you know.
You are choked, that's all.

Hurry Up, America.
I'll wait.